I0109085

100 Watt Life

No Longer Hidden. Positioned to Shine.

ANTOINE D. JACKSON

Sow Graphics & Publications, LLC | Southfield, MI

100-Watt Life
Copyright © 2013 Antoine D. Jackson
Published by Antoine D. Jackson of Sow Graphics & Publications
All rights reserved.
ISBN: 0615813496 | ISBN-13: 978-0615813493

All scripture quotations are taken from the King James Version of the
Bible, unless otherwise noted. Copyright © 1977, 1984, 2991 by
Thomas Nelson, Inc. and from The Message. Copyright © 1993, 1994,
1995, 1996, 2000, 2001, 2002. Used by permission of NavPress
Publishing Group

Cover & Interior Design: Sow Graphics & Publications, LLC
Edited by Tenita C. Johnson of So It Is Written LLC.

Printed in the United States of America

ALL RIGHTS RESERVED

No part of this book may be reproduced in any form or by any
electronic or mechanical means, including information storage and
retrieval systems, without written permission from the publisher or
author, except in the case of a reviewer, who may quote brief passages
embodied in critical articles or in a review.

DEDICATION

To Madison, you were created to be a light.
Keep shining!

DEDICATION

To Madison, you were created to be a light.
Keep shining!

CONTENTS

Acknowledgments

When I first felt the desire to write this book, I was unsure of how it would be received. While this is my second time going through this process, it feels like it's the first time. Just as before, I am thankful for the prayers, words of encouragement and the kind reviews of family and friends. I thank God for the opportunity to do what it is that I do. There are many who support me throughout the writing process as I work to bring this and other projects to the light.

I thank God for the opportunity He has afforded me with to share through writing. Writing allows me to minister to those I may never see in person. I give all praise unto you Lord for choosing me for this work and for this time. Thank you for providing all of my needs according to your riches in glory through Christ Jesus. I pray this work blesses the lives of all those that come in contact with it.

Chapter 1
Where Am I?

I enjoy driving, especially for long distances. It is therapeutic and the sightseeing is often the highlight of the trip for me. In most instances, when I set out to drive long distance, I have to ensure that I have all necessities in place. Before I take my trip, there is a routine that I commit to. Days before my departure, I have my vehicle serviced at the dealership. They check my tire pressure, tread levels, braking system, fluids and the condition of the filters and lighting system. Having all these things checked puts me at ease because now I know that the car is in tip-top shape for the trip. Now, I'm ready to travel.

Not too long ago, my family and I took a summer vacation to visit family and friends in South Carolina. The drive from our home in suburban Detroit took about eleven and a half hours. Despite the time, we were just excited about seeing our family and friends. With the car cleared by the mechanic and the gas tank on full, we packed the trunk with our luggage and belongings and buckled ourselves into our seats. We whispered a few lines of prayer for God's protection and then I grabbed my mobile phone to access the navigation application. Looking to my co-pilot for the address to my family's house, I looked down at my phone to see two options for inputting the address:

Speak Destination

Type Destination

As often as I had used the navigation app on my phone, this was the first time I noticed these two options. I had the opportunity to speak my destination or to write it. It dawned on me in that moment that just as my navigation device provided me with those options, life has as well. Essentially, the navigational system was asking me, "Where are you going?" I had the *choice* to speak it or write it.

But what is our destination? Our destination is our purpose, target, goal, and intention for our lives.

In the aforementioned instance, my family and I intended to have the car checked by the mechanic, load the

luggage and buckle ourselves in to reach a particular destination, which was South Carolina. What is your destination? As you speak and write, are you looking and keeping in mind your destination? A wise man once said, "...for *out of the abundance of the heart his mouth speaks.*" *(Luke 6:45 N KJV)* Even more, he said, *"For as he thinks in his heart, so is he."(Proverbs 23:7)* Therefore, we can conclude that if I can hear your spoken words, I can see what's in your heart. Even more, if you show me your heart, I can show you your thoughts. If you show me your thoughts, I can show you your world.

For most of us, when it comes to figuring out where to go in life, we never stop to consider the words we have spoken and written. The things we have spoken and written frame the lives we shall live. But that's just one side of this double-sided coin.

After I was given the address and I typed it into the system, there appeared another appeal. The app requested our starting point. Despite having been given the option to speak or type in our destination first, we now had to identify where we were at that moment. Although my phone is powered by satellites and can map out my route using such satellites, the requirement to proceed any further on my journey required the answering of yet another question. This time, it was a three-word question, "Where am I?"

Life is an exciting journey; one filled with ups and downs, victories and defeats, classes, lessons and exams. Oh, did I mention it is filled with work? Yet in all of this, you and I have a few choices to make. We can choose to settle into the normal status quo of life or we can choose to live lives that are thriving, flourishing, vibrant and shining. Otherwise, we may find ourselves living and going about with the humdrum behaviors and never experience the brighter side of life.

Have you ever wondered what it is that successful, thriving, flourishing, vibrant and shining people have figured out that the average man has not figured out? Perhaps they have discovered that you can speak and write your destination. Perhaps they have come to the conclusion that there is more to the world than their thirty-two block radius. Or just maybe, they have become convinced that there is a bright, shining purpose within them that longs to come out and play.

Whatever it is that they have discovered I'd like to believe that every average man would like to know. If there is some bright, illuminating thought that they have discovered, perhaps it's the thought that nothing is impossible. Maybe, just maybe, they believe they have been chosen to be lights amidst the dark, mundane and monotonous world.

Chapter 2
Time to Shine

Lights amidst the dark, mundane and monotonous world! That sounds like a line from an inspirational poem, but it's not. For years, many have attempted to describe and label the types of lives that people lead. Yet, no one has taken the time to explore the value and need for a light-exuding life. It is an unfortunate state of affairs that we never recognize the light of someone's life until it dims or goes out. Too often, I sit at funerals and memorial services, hearing people share how awesome someone *was*. The line of people ready to give their "two-minute" remarks seems to wrap the perimeter of the room. Yet, I cannot help but often wonder, in the most non-critical or judgmental way, how many of the deceased heard those accolades and words of encouragement while they lived. The saying goes, "Give me my flowers while I can smell them."

It's time that someone talked about the light while you're living. My sincerest hope is that as you read, you will become aware of the light that is within you and others. Even more, I want to encourage you to let the light within you shine. Why live life on empty or halfway when you can live at your full capacity?

Why 100 Watt Life? I immediately recognized that there are higher wattages for bulbs; yet, the 100-watt bulb is commonly used in our society. When we consider the number 100, we see its significance as well. Consider these few instances:

- In Biblical study, Abraham received his promised son at the age of 100.
- In Science, the boiling point of water is 100 Degrees Celsius
- In Business, 100 is the highest in the principle of return.

Aside from the aforementioned significance of 100, research reveals that higher wattages of bulbs are typically considered specialty bulbs and are often harder to come by. This is not the case in this instance; living a light-shining life is not hard. But it does take work and commitment.

You were put here to be a light, but not just any light. You were created to be a bright light. You were placed here on earth to live a light-exuding life. That means that you are living your life on purpose. While there are some who contend we spend our lives chasing purpose, I disagree. Why spend your life chasing something? Once I catch it, will I then get another life to enjoy it? Probably not! Therefore, we can conclude that it is insane to spend our lives chasing something that's already in front of us. Why not live on purpose *daily*? Wake up on purpose. Sing on purpose. Pray on purpose. Love your spouse on purpose. Rest on purpose. Speak the truth in love on purpose. Don't waste another minute chasing purpose. Instead, live it. That's living a light-exuding life.

When you start living on purpose, you begin to reveal the divine hues in the earth. Our task is to let our lights shine before the people so they can see our good works and give glory to our divine creator. Why spend another day, week, month, year or moment in darkness? Make up your mind to shine. Maybe you don't know quite how. By the end of this journey, you will know how to lead a life that exudes the light and reveals the divine hues to the world around us. The task is clear and straight to the point, *Let your light so shine before men, that they may see your good works and glorify your father in heaven. (Matthew*

5:16 NKJV) I know we live in a dark, merciless and grave world. But, the task remains the same.

The principles in this book will illustrate how to accomplish the task at hand. Even more, it will show you how to shine beyond the definitions imposed by traditional, religious, institutional and secular views. You will discover what it really means to shine. Caution! This book will not answer all of your questions, but it will provide direction to the answers for all of life's most challenging questions. Use the following pages as a road map to shine your light, and you will see how this applies to your entire life. Unlike other books that make promises of a life change, this book humbly offers the necessary principles, fundamentals and commitments to live a life that exudes light. I call it the 100-Watt Life.

Living this life will put our good works under the spotlight and allow them to shine for the whole world to see. However, the purpose is not for us to take the credit for what we have done. It is to lead them to the source of our strength. Your light shines to display the divine power that is on your life. I reiterate to you that this is more than just another great book to read; this is an opening to a great journey, a journey toward the light. This book will lend a hand to you as you seek to live a life that exudes the light.

If you have been feeling for some time that there is more that you are supposed to and could be doing, this book is for you. It may seem that with each day that passes, life is seemingly passing you by. You have become trapped by insecurities, doubt and a weakened faith. You have been putting dreams and visions on hold. Yet, something within you just won't give up. Despite your feelings of entrapment, you are convinced that there is more to this life than what you are currently experiencing. I'm here to lend a helping hand as you journey to find what you should, and could, be doing.

While I'm always excited to write, preach and teach, I caution that I have not arrived nor reached the pinnacle of success or my highest vibrancy. However, for reasons unbeknownst to me, God has called me to teach and preach. I often think it's because I have so much to learn. I still do. Whatever the reason, I am eager to learn more. The more I learn, the more I want to share. With that in mind, I am sharing this book as one who is pressing on the upward way.

Here are my final notes as we begin. Grab a pen, note pad and journal as you read. As you go through the various chapters, take a moment and reflect on what you've read. Reading without reflection is pointless. Besides, you can only get out what you put in. Take full advantage of this book and the information it contains. It has the potential to strengthen and even increase the reach of your light.

Chapter 3
Need for Light

A milestone moment stared me in the face.

Although I had moved into my own place before, this time was unlike the first. This time, I was moving as an adult man. Like most new adults, I anticipated this moment. The moment when you enter a new place of residence you've invested, worked and sacrificed to acquire. With the key in hand, I ventured down the stairs and through the door that led to the hallway of the first floor, and there it was. The sign on the roughly painted brown door read: "A1."

I turned the key into the lock. Hearing the moving mechanisms of the deadbolt brought elation to my heart. Finally, I felt the slight vibration as the lock exited the wall through the door frame and the once stiff door moved.

There I was, entering a brand new apartment with my wife.

Excited and filled with emotion, my hand reached inside the dark room, feeling for a light switch. Along the left wall, there was one. Grasping it and moving it in the upward position, the darkness remained. Convinced that there was problem, I sat down the box that was in my hand. I proceeded to the wall straight ahead, depending on the light from the hallway. Yes, another light switch. Grasping the plastic switch, with seemingly all my might, I pushed it upward. And there was light!

In similar fashion, you may have had to enter some dark, unlit rooms a few times in your life. The first thought in your mind was to turn on some light. This seems like the logical and instinctive thing to do. After all, it is a dark room. These regular life experiences teach us some valuable lessons. The first lesson is that our entrance into the room reveals the existence of a lack. There is a lack of light. Where there is a lack, there is also another element at play: a need. This is the second lesson.

My entrance into the dark room revealed that there was not only a lack of light, but a *need* for light. All too often, we realize there is a state of lack. But we also fail to realize that a lack is nothing short of a need. For example, when you finally discover that your spouse used the last of the toilet tissue and did not replace the roll, that discovery was prompted probably in the moment that you needed the tissue. The identification of lack happens in the time of need.

The third lesson to take away from this is that we don't realize a need quickly because we have not recognized purpose. In the instance of my entering of the apartment, I was there for a purpose. A wise man once said, *To everything there is a season, and a time to every purpose under the heaven: (Ecclesiastes 3:1 KJV).* While all things have seasons, purpose has been given time. So when purpose shows up, it immediately gets to work. The establishing of purpose will reveal what is lacking. In the instance of my entering the apartment, my purpose caused light to become a necessity and because I had purpose, it revealed the lack in the room. I needed light in order to reach my purpose.

Write this down. Purpose is the precondition to the entrance of light. A life without purpose is a life without light. A life without light is a life without purpose. The good news is that our purpose was established long before we reached the earthly world we now live in. Our purpose was in mind at the time of creation. We discover our purpose only when we come into connection with the divine source. Our purpose was set before time began and we need the light to fulfill it.

The Need Remains

Since the beginning of time, we have observed a need for light. From the time of creation until now, the need remains. The earth was without form and void and darkness covered everything. The words 'let there be light' were spoken and so it was. The infinite one in His wisdom began His dressing of the heavens and earth by clothing it with light. After clothing the earth and the heavens with light, a separation had to be made between light and darkness. This was only the beginning of light's existence. Throughout our human existence, man has worked tirelessly to improve upon the existence of light. The efforts continue to strengthen the distinction between light and darkness. The tireless work continued because there had become an established and recognized need for light. Purpose was revealed and light was needed to fulfill purpose.

Let's look at how early civilizations found comfort in innovative ways to light up the dark. When we consider many of the ancient writings and other artifacts that have gained notoriety and fame in our present day, we see the value of having light. Light allows for the creativity of man to flow and come to fruition. Many of the ancient artifacts were created under the glow of a torch, a lantern or perhaps a lit candlestick. The evolution of oil-based lamps, lanterns, etc. maintains the existence of a need for light and this existence has been because of the need. Can you imagine that the first computer, calculator or iPhone® was constructed under the glow of a light, possibly a 100-watt bulb? In our society today, we continue to see innovative designs, practices and uses of light because there remains a constant need for light. The need for light is observed in all facets of our lives, both spiritual and natural.

We live in a dark world. We need more light. Our society has fallen into what some might consider a repeat of the dark ages; however, this time, it's a spiritual darkness that has led to intellectual and economic regression. Political unrest, violence, strife, robbery, and all other manners of evil have seemingly darkened the lights of our world. There is a need for light. This has not changed. Not just the light of a 100-watt bulb. Instead, we need the light of our lives to shine through in the world. But how will this light reach the world? Will God come down Himself and light the world? While we know nothing is impossible to Him, He gives us the answer. No. Instead, it is plainly written that we, you and I, are to be the vessels of light in the world. So the light that is needed is the light of our lives.

When I entered my new apartment and experienced the momentary absence of light, I wonder how things might have happened had I not finally turned on some light. Maybe I would have stumbled over the boxes that had already been delivered. Possibly, my wife would have jammed her toe against the couch that sat in the living room. The truth of the matter is that whatever we would have done would have been influenced by the absence of light.

Making choices in the dark can lead to some undesirable penalties. Therefore, we discern that just as in the natural we need the light, so it is in the spiritual. Light is important to our daily human and spiritual lives. No one would willingly walk an unfamiliar path without some light. Let's not be crazy; let's get the light. You and I are called to be the lights of the world. Our design is exude the light in this dark world. We must shine.

Chapter 4
Empowered to Shine

There I was sitting on the fifty yard line in a professional sporting arena, dressed in full graduation regalia. My mind began to wander back to the "top porch" of the three-family unit house where I grew up. It was there that I did a great deal of my daydreaming. I would daydream about what my future would be. I dreamed about the type of car I would drive, the clothes I would wear, and the type of person that I would become. The imagery in my mind became intoxicating and, for a long time, all I wanted was to have some of those images leave the confines of my mind and manifest before my eyes.

The day I graduated with my undergraduate degree was one of the times that I felt the daydreams of my past had traveled to the present. That day, I sat in what used to be a dream. The images once confined to my mind had manifest before my eyes. I was overcome with gratitude, knowing that the journey to reach that place was one of the most challenging I had ever encountered.

In the face of insurmountable odds, I made history for my family and myself. What should have been a four or five-year journey had evolved into nine years of hard work and dedication. I see now that this was a journey that required commitment far beyond what I expected.

After walking across the stage and receiving that rolled up piece of paper with instructions on how to obtain my actual degree, the phrase, *"Empowered to make it happen,"* leaped from my lips. To the naked eye, the rolled up piece of paper was what I had spent nine years to acquire. But on the contrary, it was the information inscribed on that paper that gave me empowerment.

Still reciting the phrase, my mind was racing. Recognizing it was more than just a cliché, I hurried to my seat to write it down. As I did, a fellow classmate said, "I think you just got the title to your next book." Laughing it off, I tucked the paper square into my shirt pocket and stood waiting on the formal conferring of my degree.

Later that day, while talking and celebrating, the phrase continuously found its way into just about every conversation. Looking back, I believe that the single most important part of that statement was that I was *empowered.* But, empowered to do what?

Growing up in a traditionally African American Christian home, I was taught that in order to succeed, you needed to have a personal relationship with God, the source of empowerment. You had to be empowered.

My grandmother faithfully got us up for church and demanded that we attend Sunday school. Man, how I disliked those early mornings! Despite my disdain, before I knew it, church had become an outlet to endless possibilities for me. I discovered that through God anything was possible and that with Him, I was possible. It didn't take long to figure out that having a relationship with Christ empowered me. Yet, I still had not discovered what I was empowered to do.

The initial discovery of my empowerment ushered me into my present motivation. I became intoxicated with sharing, with everyone that I encountered, the beauty of having a personal relationship with God and the power that He has to transform our lives. He can transform our lives into light-exuding lives. That was it; I had been empowered to shine. Yes, my life had become empowered to shine and serve as a beacon, leading others to the source of my empowerment. My good works would be highlighted and I could tell others how I got there.

The nine-year journey through undergraduate school revealed to me what was within me the whole time. The rolled up paper signified the completion of that portion of my journey and access to my next level. To the naked eye, that was simply a rolled up paper with writing on it held together by a simple ribbon. But, there is more than meets the eye. The words on that paper authorized me, sanctioned me, and empowered me to reach a destination.

In similar fashion, with each new day comes the authorization, sanctioning and empowering of us to shine before man in every area of our lives. We have been given the needed resources, talents, abilities and qualities. So why aren't we shining? For far too long, we have hidden our lights and kept secret our talents and abilities. We must know today that we have been empowered to make it happen. Shine. When a lamp is plugged in, it becomes operational and capable of illumination. When connected to God, we become empowered to shine. But, just as my graduation day epiphany revealed, there is a process for us to discover our empowerment.

The process for empowerment to shine requires that we not conform to those around us, nor the systems presented. Instead, we are to become transformed.

The transformation begins within our minds and secondly, in our hearts. Both our heart and mind must be renewed and cleansed so that we can shine the divine hues in the world in which we live.

The process of empowerment, while thought to be short, takes a lifetime; however, even as our power levels are being built up, we can still shine. Through the right connection, you have been empowered to shine.

Chapter 5
Chosen to Shine

Not only are you empowered to shine, but you've been chosen to shine. I heard a preacher say once, "We give too much credit to our enemies and haters." As he presented his argument, I could not help but to agree with him. It is true that the world we live in finds it easier to ridicule than to encourage, easier to condemn than to uplift and easier to hate than to love. Perhaps this has more to do with the psychological makeup of humans.

According to several notable psychologists, the human mind, when introduced to new activities or concepts, produces A.N.T.'s. No, it's not the small little species known for invading a pitcher of lemonade on a hot summer's day. These A.N.T.'s are automatic negative thoughts. Even I suffer from this condition from time to time. Automatic negative thoughts often show up in our lives in the form of doubt, self-destructive behavior and the absence of faith. Have you ever shared a great idea with someone, only to have them find every fault with it? Or perhaps, you decided to finally write your book. The moment you sat at the computer to begin typing, suddenly your mind became inundated with every reason why you *couldn't* write the book. Do you suffer from A.N.T.'s? No worries! There is a cure for this disorder. It's called faith.

The thought of shining your light could be terrifying to you. You may find it intimidating to shine. Yet, those who live light-exuding lives must know that not everyone or even you will readily appreciate your light. In fact, the most common response is to resort to evil and hatred-filled communication. This only happens because you made the decision to shine. When you decide to move from status quo to extraordinary, you will attract self-inflicted and outside assaults.

When this happens, be of good cheer. It means that you are knocking on the unlocked door of your purpose. You may find that the world will not like you because you have sold out to your purpose (to shine) and have opted to do something that they are not willing to do.

The world has been waiting for you. Believe it or not, the world can often see the light in us before we can.

Consequently, there are some who will make (hopefully unsuccessful) attempts to hinder our progress. When you have recognized the light that exudes, your thinking, living, seeing and speaking are transformed. The transformation to this place of enlightenment is not based on arrogance and pompous behavior. It is, however, a transformation rooted in genuine love and respect for us and others. Living a light-exuding life is not a license to go around boasting of ourselves or thinking of ourselves more highly than others. In this life, we should avoid the pride and entitlement trap at all cost. In all of this, there is a silent challenge in being chosen.

Even though we've been selected, and even hand-picked, the challenge becomes remaining humble. Take the biblical patriarch David for example. He was one of the most memorable kings who served over Israel. David was selected as king over Israel long before his reign began. He was chosen for the kingship even while Saul, the reigning king, was still on the throne. Samuel, the prophet, went down to Jesse's house because he was told he would find the next king of Israel there.

After Samuel observed each of Jesse's children and inquired of God who was the next king, God plainly spoke to him and let him know that none of them were the chosen one. This amazes me. God is so meticulous and specific, despite the fact that He created so much and so many. He knows each of us by name and even knows the number of hairs on our head. Jesse, possibly looking confused and maybe even saddened at the prophet's declaration, remembers that he has one more son. He reluctantly called for David, his youngest son, to be brought in from the field. At that moment, it became clear that God had chosen him to be the next king.

We find that it was years later that he actually reigned as king over Israel. Nonetheless, throughout his journey, he never became arrogant, pompous or prideful.

Preparation & Performance

The principle that we learn from David's life is one of importance. As we go on to live light-exuding lives, we must come to grips with the truth that God has us in one of two seasons: a season of preparation or a season of performance.

The season of preparation can be seen as the time when we are out in the field working with our father's sheep, defending our flocks from lions and bears. In our season of preparation, we are assigned the task of delivering lunch to others as they do battle. It is even in our time of preparation that we defeat giants. Our season of preparation is the time allotted for us to be molded, developed, strengthened and groomed. Our habits, issues and struggles are addressed at this phase. Are you in a season of preparation?

In comparison, the season of performance is that time when you exercise the calling, gifting and abilities you learned and received in the field. In your season of performance, you will lead people to victory, and you'll become a guide to others. In the season of performance, the giants that once had you grappling in fear are now intimidated by you. In this season, you spend little time being concerned over your enemies. In your season of performance, you will triumph over adversity and restore the important things that lead to destiny and purpose. David exhibits preparation and performance through his journey to the kingship.

The Timing of Choice

The fact that David was chosen to be king while Saul was still on the throne did not occur by happenstance. Divine timing is often not in accordance with ours. The beauty of being chosen to shine is that it is not limited to time. Before the worlds were framed, the choice was already made. Prior to the error of our ways, the fear, the anger and the lies, the choice for you and I to shine was made. Jeremiah 1:5 says, *"Before I formed thee in the belly I knew thee; and before thou camest forth out of the womb I sanctified thee, and I ordained thee a prophet unto the nations."* We were chosen because we have purpose.

Leading a light-exuding life requires a good foundation. Essential to this foundation is the knowledge of the choice that has been made. You have been chosen to shine and show forth the divine hues in the earth. Ensure that your light is strong, vibrant and long-lasting during your season of performance. Know that the timing is perfect. The good work that was started in you will be finished. You were chosen for this.

Chapter 6
Positioned to Shine

Would you take a perfectly good lamp, plug it into an outlet, sit it on the floor and place it behind a chair? That was the question I asked myself when I got home from school that Thursday afternoon. My grandmother took the lamp shade off the top of the lamp stand, and placed the illuminating lamp on the floor behind the chair. Calling out for her, she raised her head from the other side of the chair and said, "Here I am." I wondered what she was doing. But before I could inquire, she said, "I dropped my needle behind this chair and I'm trying to find it." Breathing a sigh of relief, I dropped my book bag and got down on all fours to help her find the needle.

Years later, when I reflect on that incident and consider how our lives are to be light-exuding lives, I imagine that just as my grandmother had reasoning for positioning the lamp, there is great reasoning for positioning us as light in the earth. My grandmother needed the light to find her lost needle, which had fallen somewhere on the floor. Similar to that needle, there are things missing that have fallen into the dark abyss of this world. This is where the light is truly needed. A vibrant, rightly positioned light is needed to lead people and things back into order. We as light bearers are the ones who should be positioned to help.

Our lives must exude the divine hues in the earth. We were not given lights only to have them hidden under bushels, buckets and behind chairs. We have been illuminated and positioned for all to see. What good is a flashlight in a dark room if it's inside of a bag? What good is a lighthouse that is covered by mountains? We are a city on a hill that cannot be hid. The light of our lives should illuminate so much that it is impossible to hide.

We have become endowed with a power to do things that are beyond our own physical and mental abilities. It's time to do the good works and shine. Our lives should exude light to the world around us. It shouldn't be hidden. The light of our lives should shine forth. We have been set as a city on a hill, a candle on a candlestick, and a light on a light stand. It's time that we go public with our light. It is time to stop operating in hidden purpose and secret faith. It's time to shine.

The 100-watt life is a life that has been positioned to shine. Whether we're in our homes, communities or places of employment, we are expected to shine.

Despite the lamp's seemingly outrageous position, it still managed to shine. We must be committed to shining wherever we've been placed. We cannot pick and choose where we will shine. We cannot turn it off and on. Our light offers hope to others. Shine forth your purpose. Shine forth your good works.

Chapter 7

Flip the Switch or Change the Bulb

Now, the real work begins. A good friend of mine's who is a pastor said, "Inspiration without information is ignorance on fire." There is too much good in us to let it burn in ignorance.

In the earlier chapters, we learned that there is a need for light. We learned just how important this need is in our lives. We also learned that we have been empowered, chosen and positioned to shine. This information has served as building blocks to our foundation. However, there is more to be added before you can build.

Now that we've done some excavating, framing and pouring foundation, it's time we add some height to our building. Anyone can talk about exuding light. It's the implementation of the exuding that is such a hassle. For many of us, we don't wake up with a mind to live aimlessly. In fact, most of us go to bed and wake up with the sincerest of all intentions to be, and do, better. The reality is that we often don't know *how* to do better. Action always beats intention. So let's take action and shine.

In the next chapters, we will discover the characteristics of the 100-watt life and how to apply them to strengthen our light-exuding lives.

REMINDER: Grab a pen and pad to take notes as you read and jot down inspirational thoughts that flood your mind as you read. At the end of each chapter, take a moment and reflect on what you've read, and set a goal to display that characteristic in your life. Small steps in the right direction take us further than we could ever imagine. Small shifts move big ships.

Don't be afraid or feel intimidated if you have not been exhibiting some or all of the characteristics described. It takes a moment for a bulb to reach its highest luminosity. It is not until after the coils warm up that the inner parts begin to respond. Let these chapters serve as a reminder and motivation to shine every day, everywhere, in every moment.

But before we dive in, there is an elephant in the room you must confront. His name is *fear*. Fear is the one thing that, if not dealt with properly, can destroy your chances of ever living a 100-watt life. Fear is an emotional response that all people exhibit. It comes upon us in times of great stress, strain and growth. If and when left unchecked, fear can immobilize, terrorize, and ostracize.

Fear is a double-minded character. It never really makes up its mind about anything. It is unstable in all of its ways. Fear is counterproductive. It exists solely to go against attempted productivity. Living a light-exuding life requires us to deal with fear head on. One strategy for dealing with fear is to question it. The next time you sit to write your book, ask fear why it won't work. The next time you get up to sing a song, see what fear says as a reason why you shouldn't. When you prepare to ask the beautiful woman in apartment 4B out on a date and fear shows up, ask fear what disqualifies you. Fear, when exposed, never remains. Too often, we live our lives exposed to fear. Instead, expose fear to the light of your life. Flip the switch or change the bulb. But whatever you do, make up your mind to shine. There is too much darkness in our world to remain hidden and in secret. Take your rightful positions and be about your assignment in the earth. Let's shine!

Chapter 8
Self Limiting Thoughts

The title of this chapter sounds like a fancy psychological term used to diagnose someone who constantly thinks negatively. While I cannot say that it is or isn't a psychological condition, I can attest to my life being plagued by self-limiting thoughts. Self-limiting thoughts are those that focus on the negative instead of the positive. Typically, these types of thoughts arise when you make a decision to try something new, start a business or write a book.

The reality is that self-limiting thoughts are about you and can be heard only by you. These thoughts are always far from the truth and your reality. These are the baby elephants that were produced by the big elephant discussed in the previous chapter: fear. Birthed out of fear, self-limiting thoughts find and present a strong case for why you *can't* do something. You know you are allowing self-limiting thoughts to lead you if you spend a lot of time thinking what could go wrong.

I remember the day that I decided to write my first book. The adrenaline that my body produced at that moment took me to a new level of excitement. I sat at my laptop and started typing. However, before I could save the first paragraph, my mind became inundated with worry and self-argument. *How can you write a book? You've never done this before. Who said you were qualified to write? It takes years to write and successfully publish a book. Are you ready to invest thousands of dollars into this idea?* The questions seemed to argue both sides of the coin. *What if the book does well? How will you travel and host signings, and still be a good husband and father? What will you do for employment? You can't travel and work a nine to five.* Fear had officially set in.

Learn to analyze the worry. Any great idea brings with it a degree of worry and anxiety. However, we can come up with a plan of action to deal with the worry. While worry should never be the focus of your day, don't allow worry to immobilize you from shining; deal with it head on. This, of course, takes patience, prayer and more patience. Not to mention, you'll need a hefty dose of courage.

Being courageous is one of the requirements of living a 100-watt life; however, you must also be courageous in your fight against self-limiting thoughts. Combating self- limiting thoughts will take focus. Adjusting your focus to what you want to accomplish and not the outcomes, or even the process, alienates those self-limiting thoughts. While they will not quickly go away, similar to a garden lacking water, they will die. Adjusting your focus enables you to hone in on the project or task at hand and instead of the potential challenges that could arise. This doesn't mean you are nonchalant about the potential risk; you just take the power away from the risk. Living your life in view of the potential risk will lead to life in a bubble. You'll never enjoy the fullness of your talents, gifts and abilities and you'll never shine.

Jot down a few of the self-limiting thoughts you hear in your mind. Then, analyze each thought. Determine if the thought has any validity. Ask yourself if the self-limiting thought can possibly occur, and then come up with a strategy on how to avoid it. For those thoughts that you find are far reaching and asinine, simply write them down and trash them. I have discovered that when I shine the light on my self-limiting thoughts, they typically end up in the trash and the mental anguish that they once caused dissipates.

Chapter 9
Growth: Not Optional

In my life, prayer and meditation are the places where I overcome self-limiting thoughts. Even more, prayer and meditation is where I discover the need for further growth and development. As with all growth and development, one must desire and be willing to go through the process.

Living a 100-watt life requires a commitment to grow up. It seems harsh, but the reality is immaturity will only breed immaturity. This reminds me of my daughter, Madison. One evening, I walked into her room only to discover that she had taken nearly every toy that she has out of the toy bin and scattered them all over the floor. When I asked her why the toys were out, she looked up at me with those big pretty eyes and replied, "I'm playing with them." Forced into submission by her raspy voice and innocent face, I turned and walked back to the living room and resumed my work at the computer. Later that evening, I went into her room to find that she had put all but three or four toys back in the bin. I smiled and called for her to come in the room. I asked her what happened to all of the toys she had out earlier. She replied, "I'm done playing, so I put the toys away." Needless to say, I was extremely proud of her efforts and her maturity to know that when she was done, the toys needed to be put away.

The experience caused me to think a little further on how awesome it is when we reach such a place in our lives. Living a 100-watt life requires growth. The task is to "let our light shine" for all to see. There are several synonyms for the word let, including to allow, to give permission, permit to and agree to. The growth required for a light-exuding life is a place of maturity, a place where we are no longer tossed to and fro, indulged or coddled. In this place, we are no longer bothered by the bickering, griping and hateful words, or gestures and feelings of others spewed toward us. Our focus is elsewhere. We are no longer children, but we are grown-ups. The writer in 1 Corinthians 13:11 encouraged the people to reflect on the coming maturation and development as they grow. He wrote, *When I was a child, I spoke as a child, I understood as a child, I thought as a child: but when I became a man, I put away childish things.* The writer knew that the current state of the people of Corinth was a state of childhood and immaturity; however, he encouraged them to look forward to a future adulthood. The plea of this missionary to the people at Corinth reverberates in our ears today as we pursue a 100-watt life: "Put away the childish things."

Children have slender views, cluttered philosophies and blurred thinking. Such immaturity should not be named among adults. However, sadly enough, most of us know adults who act more like children than they do adults. Just as a child has temper tantrums, their thinking is severely blurred and they have slender views. They are not leading a light-exuding life.

A life that exudes light is a life that appreciates and welcomes maturity. We must examine our lives to see if we are able to handle the light we are seeking. While the thought is that most light bulb sockets are universal, they aren't. Warning labels on lamps inform us of which measure of bulb wattage they can accommodate. So we must examine ourselves to see if we have grown to be able to carry the light. We must ask ourselves four poignant questions:

1. Can my life accommodate the 100-watt light?

2. Is my infrastructure able to withstand the growth and pressure that comes along with it?

3. Has my mind been transformed and my heart renewed to exude this light?

4. Have I grown up?

In 1 Corinthians, the writer warned the people not to carry forth the childlike temperaments. He even presents them with a challenge. The challenge can be observed in his use of perhaps the most important word in the writing: I. The writer's challenge to the people was to personally make a decision to put away childish things. He even affirms that he also was once a child, spoke as a child, and understood as a child.

The single most significant threat to growth is the inability to admit your lack thereof. Failure to own up to where we are is the first step down a path of no return. Yet, there are still other threats to growth that we must be watchful of. Those threats are pride and laziness.

There is hope that we can overcome. The writer provides us a litmus test in determining our level of growth and maturity. He contends that our childlike behaviors can and will be observed in our appearance, speech, understanding and thoughts. People who live light-exuding lives will take time to examine themselves.

The writer's declaration that, "I became a man" leads me to believe that to mature is a matter of one's own choice. Even more, the statement of, "I put away childish things" exhibits the responsibility placed upon each of us to go after maturity. Nowhere did he say that he was forced to put them away, nor does he give reference to someone taking them away. On the contrary, the writer shows us that he made an informed decision to put away the speech, understanding and thoughts of immaturity and childishness.

If you're done playing, it's time to put the toys away. Relinquish the childish speech, understanding and thoughts!

The light-exuding life is one where growth is not an option; it's a must. This light can only be experienced in the life of those who have taken on the needed maturity. Those living a light-exuding life understand the continued need to focus on living on purpose. Furthermore, they see a need to live with increased passion. Living a light-exuding life does not mean that you've outgrown the basics of faith. Instead, it means you recognize that the basics are really the essentials. Our continued growth in life will strengthen our connection to the source and cause our light to become vibrant and unwavering. We then illuminate the world around us with maturity, stability and promise.

Chapter 10
Commit to Shine

Going after a light-exuding life makes you hope and dream beyond where you presently are. In my hopes and dreams, there are many things in this world that I'd like to do. Some of those things include traveling the world, seeing the pyramids and enjoying my latter years with peace, good health and my family.

Beyond that, I'd like to one day visit each of the continents and take a visit to outer space. All the same, I recognize that none of these things can be accomplished without me putting into practice the age old art of commitment. I have discovered that most people want things without the commitment. For this reason, most mobile service providers offer or have a subsidiary that offers "no contract" plans. The number of persons renting a home is ten times the number of those who own a home.

We want huge savings and investment account balances, but we will not commit to decreasing our frivolous spending habits. We desire sincere and growing relationships, but we won't commit to spending quality time with our mates or loved ones. We want the harvest without the labor. But harvesting is labor-intensive. Too many of us want something for nothing.

Our modern-day society has become afraid of commitment. There are many people who are in a relationship or dating, and choose to cohabitate. Yet, when asked about marriage (a commitment), they are hesitant. We live in a society where commitment has become the new curse word. Most of our society operates with what I call the "3M" mentality. No, not the mentality of the lucrative office product manufacturer. I'm talking about the Mine, Microwave and Mall mentality.

People with the mine mentality say that they are concerned about no one else but themselves or those that belong to them. You've probably heard the "my four and no more" statement. Those with the microwave mentality want everything quick, fast and in a hurry. They have no time to wait and refuse to be denied what they want. Then you have those with the mall mentality. They want to have nothing to do with commitment. This perhaps is the paramount of the "3M" mentality in our world today. A shopping mall gives you choice without commitment. You can go to the mall and shop one of many stores with no commitment to any specific store. When one fails you, you simply leave and head to another store. Those with the mall mentality apply this thinking to every area of their lives. Much of our society falls into one, if not all, of these categories.

There is a great need for commitment in our world. Someone has to be committed to seeing our children do better in school. Someone has to be committed to ensuring our seniors live healthy and productive latter years. Someone has to be committed to seeing marriages between one man and one woman survives. We need commitment. The absence of commitment creates an environment where anything goes. In the absence of commitment, chaos, disunity and unfaithfulness become the order of the day. Nothing is sacred and at the drop of a dime, you can excuse yourself from a situation, relationship or responsibility. If we are to live lives that exude light, we must become people of commitment.

Cornel West, author of *Breaking Bread: Insurgent Black Intellectual Life* and noted scholar stated, "We have to recognize that there cannot be relationships unless there is commitment, unless there is loyalty, unless there is love, patience, persistence."

As displayed in Dr. West's statement, commitment leads to the need for much more. It is often this truth that intimidates some, so they run away from commitment because of the inability to perform the subsequent tasks. Our level of commitment to a person, task or way will always be viewed in the final output.

Living a life that exudes light requires us to be committed. In every facet of our lives, we must have a commitment. When we begin a journey and then turn back, we become unfit for leadership roles and places of dominion. There is leadership and dominion in light-exuding lives.

Our level of commitment will forecast the liveliness of our light. In a life that exudes light, three essential commitments are needed: a commitment to purpose, commitment to good works and commitment to shine. We must be committed to the light and the purpose that has been to given us.

Chapter 11
Get Some Help

I'm committed to being an entrepreneur and have been for more than ten years. As an entrepreneur and working professional, I have learned many lessons. Not all of them have been taught through traditional classroom settings either. Many of the lessons that I've learned have been presented in real life "on-the-job training sessions." Unquestionably, one of the greatest lessons that I learned was that it is beyond my aptitude to do everything. I must confess that this was a tough pill to swallow, especially because I am an entrepreneur and have the spirit of a go-getter.

At the start of my business, I had no employees. To delegate tasks to. Everything that needed to be done had to be done by me. The truth is that many of the limitations facing my business at its infancy could have been avoided had I learned the art of collaboration. The struggles of trying to run a startup business by myself taught me a hard lesson. I learned that trying to do everything leads to the accomplishment of nothing.

The world is ever changing. Much of what we do today in education, business and in our personal lives is done via the internet or other electronic devices. These changes offer a great opportunity for collaboration that increases proficiency, outcomes and profits. Collaboration also improves and extends our individual reach.

Even Jesus, the greatest man to ever live, used a collaboration to complete His work. At the onset of earthly ministry, He took time to identify and solicit persons with whom He could work to carry out His mission. He solicited those who possessed the skills needed to make it happen. The men selected had varying skills. Some were fisherman, tent makers and even tax collectors. Each of these men brought something different to the table. But together, they were able to turn the world upside down.

Our lights are intended to shine before others so that they can observe and see our good works. Our light-exuding lives should show them our good works and cause them to want to join us. As light bearers, we must learn how to collaborate with others to carry out the assignments on our lives. How foolish is it for us to detest, refuse or dismiss help? We are mutually supporting beings by nature. As a nonprofit professional, I see firsthand the value of collaboration. But sadly, I see oftentimes when it fails. Collaborations often fail because some bright person decides that, "If you come with your fifty percent and my fifty percent, then we'll be whole." This is so far from the truth. True collaboration requires all parties to come to the table with one hundred percent of their talents, gifts and abilities. Be careful; not everyone is equipped for collaboration. Use wisdom and seek direction before committing to collaboration. If we are going to lead a life that exudes light, we must be prepared to work with others.

Our commission to shine is to be done before men so that they may see our good works. Our lights are to be lit and placed so that others can see them. Once our light is seen, it will attract other light--people who are poised and committed to work. This drawing together will allow us to exude greater amounts of light into our world.

The spirit of collaboration is rooted in the very essence of a light-exuding life. Light is complementary. Collaboration works in harmony with light. To lead a light-exuding life, we must be open and receptive to collaboration. By doing so, we will accomplish the appointed vision.

Chapter 12
Hunter & Cook

It's awful to have a great product, but never take the time to market it. Many people think that their product will sell itself. That is not true at all. Companies with any good product or service have an equally good marketing plan. In addition, manufacturers or creators were not slothful in their handling of their product.

A wise man once said, *"The slothful man roasted not that which he took in hunting: but the substance of a diligent man is precious." (Proverbs 12:27 KJV)* The care and concern you show for your product can be seen in the amount of time you invest in it. In the parable, we see a man who has obviously spent some time hunting. Perhaps his hunt was prompted by his hunger. No matter what the reason, the parable states that because of his slothfulness, he does not roast that which he hunted.

I was like that guy when my first book, *When You've Had Enough: A Word on Breaking Free,* was released. I spent months working on that book. I invested time and money into the project. I took numerous amounts of time away from my family to draft it. Even though the book was published and available via my website and Amazon®, I was still not ready to roast. While some of it was fear, a great majority of it was slothfulness. Radio show hosts called to interview me about the book, and I slothfully returned calls. The elegantly written press release opened the door to television appearances and speaking engagements. Yet, I was slothful in keeping my supply of books stocked and by the time the opportunities came, I had no product available for sale.

Why have a light and hide it under a bushel? It was made for a purpose. You went hunting for the job, but now you are being slothful in your performance. You prayed day in and day out for a mate, yet you spend most of your time complaining to your friends about how awful they are. Why become a hunter and hunt, but not a cook for that which you hunted? If you want people to know that you are serious about your good works, began taking action. The wise man stated, *The substance of the diligent man is precious.* The only thing that made the hunter's and the diligent man's substance different was what they did with it once it was caught. What have you done with what you caught?

People are probably used to you coming up with new ideas and concepts. Sadly, they have become accustomed to you not cooking them. Spouses and immediate family are usually the first to experience this dissatisfaction. They watch us spend nights and weekends working on a new business plan, book project or building personalized dog houses. The initial work looks great and the excitement of the moment is contagious. However, after a few weeks, they notice that you've left the business plan underneath the coffee table, the book manuscript has ketchup and the grease stains of McDonald's® fries, and the building project sits void of its carpenter. It's time to invest. Invest time and attention to the good works you desire, but be mindful that it is not an investment at the expense of others. As I prepared to work on this book, I made certain that, because I did not cook the first book, that I invested my own time. Instead of asking my family for a leave of absence from the dinner table to write, I stayed up later and woke up earlier. Instead of writing a page or two during lunch at work, I worked through my lunch on work assignments and spent my evenings and a few vacation days writing. In a nutshell, the investment has to be a sacrifice on your part and not that of your spouse and family.

Moving from being just a great hunter requires discipline, focus and sacrifice. The greater your investment, the greater your return! Living a light-exuding life means that you've got to roast what you've hunted. What good ideas are lying dormant in your mind because you refuse to roast them? Your slothfulness to roast is affecting someone else from making it to their next level. Lives that exude light are those that hunt, kill and roast. You discover the ideas, dissect the business plan, and cook. When is the last time you cooked something?

Chapter 13
Needles & Drugs

It seems that everyone everywhere has an idea. No matter where you turn, someone is promoting and pushing their new-found idea and concept. The wave of entrepreneurship and small business startups is off the charts. Yet, for over half of the products introduced into the market annually, they fail. Perhaps they didn't cook them. The traction needed to take the product or idea to the next level of the product life cycle is never achieved. Perhaps the answer can be found in the work of the community drug dealer.

I grew up in an impoverished neighborhood in Detroit, where drugs, violence and prostitution were the norm. The most common things in our community were police cars, body bags and druggies trying to get their next fix. One of the pillars in the community outside of the church, however, was the drug man. He was, as I remember him, a family man. He was married and had a wonderful-looking wife. He had children and everyone wanted to be their friends.

PUSH THE DRUG, NOT THE NEEDLE

The drug man was never seen actively engaging in drug activity. But, all who knew the neighborhood knew he was the source for drugs. As a child, I often watched in suspense as the cops raided the known drug house and even the drug man's house. But the drug man never got arrested. Traditionally, those who were arrested were those caught with drug paraphernalia-- the equipment, supplies and tools needed to manufacture or distribute the drugs. I always wondered how this guy managed to stay in business. How did he maintain his staunch clientele? Furthermore, how did he stay out of the limelight of the police? Chances are, you have never seen a drug dealer on the corner selling syringes, spoons and saucepans. Those items are of least concern to the drug dealer because his goal is not to provide you with the equipment or tools to use the drugs; his goal is to provide you with the drug. Yes, even the drug man can teach business owners, pastors and motivational speakers a lesson. Push the drug, not the needle.

People who have embraced the 100-watt life understand that their role in the world is to be that of one pushing a drug. Our drug of choice however is the light. The motivation of the community drug dealer is money. He stands on the corner day after day, for hours on end, with the intended purpose of pushing the drugs. The consequence of him pushing the drug is increased pockets. Perhaps during the course of the day, he is asked for needles and spoons. But all he truly has to offer is the drug.

What have you failed to push because you have been focused too long on the supplies and not the product? Your gifts and talents are your supplies. Business, ministry and organizational success can be observed in those who push their product instead of the supplies. When Ford® comes up with a new car design, it is not likely that you will see a commercial from them advertising the engine alone. The engine is a tool they are using to make their product better, but it's not their product.

Light-exuding lives push the light into the world. Similar to lightening bugs on torchlight, those that want the light will be attracted to it. The light-exuding life is not concerned with making a name for themselves or even building a reputation. It is concerned with solely pushing the light. All of our effort, strength and power is given to shining our light. Push the light.

Chapter 14
Shine Creatively

I once heard a venture capitalist say that kindergarten children were asked on their first day of school how many of them were creative. Every hand in the room went up into the air, self-declaring that they were creative. After following them throughout their school career, the group of students, now high school seniors, were asked the same question. Only a mere two percent of the group considered themselves creative.

Every human being has the ability to be creative. Unlike other talents and abilities, creativity is innate. Even more, creativity can be learned by observing others. However, too often, creativity is hindered by those we surround ourselves with. We have been made in the likeness and image of God; the one that created the earth, made the sun, moon, stars and firmaments. So why are we not creative?

What happened to those students and their once high level of creativity? Perhaps the educational system has failed these children. It is no secret that the educational system in many of our communities is in dire straits. When we drill down to already challenged communities, the picture becomes even bleaker. The reason that the system is failing our children is because it does more to zap our children of creativity than it does to promote and celebrate creativity. The end result is the lack of creativity in our children. Education has, for far too long, been designed in such a manner that it restricts a student instead of freeing a student.

The light is a freeing light. It frees us to be creative in the work that has been set at our hands. We are to let our light so shine before men that they will see our "good works." One writer says that these good works are our moral excellence, and our praiseworthy and noble deeds.

The world in which we live in acknowledges creativity and innovation. Think about the legacy of the late Steve Jobs. His name continues to ring synonymous in the media because of his creativity and innovative ideals and approaches to technology. The world desires to see creativity.

As light-exuding people, we are to use creativity to our benefit. The good works that we shall perform will come about through our use of creativity. Creativity will draw the attention of man. Much of what is missing in the lives of so many is not money, time, or the prowess to be successful. What is missing is creativity! Creativity is the single most needed attribute in business and its need spans across all industries.

Consider for a moment the numerous businesses, individuals or organizations that have suffered bankruptcy, forced liquidation, closure or demise. I imagine that in more than eighty-five percent of the cases, creativity, had it been employed proactively, might have saved the business.

Even still, business, religious, civic and government professionals agree that the one trait lacking in these sectors is creativity. It's time to ignite the hearts and minds of others and impress upon them the need and desire for creativity.

We suggest and promote that they go after the life that exudes light. We were created by a creative God. We were made in the likeness and image of a creative being. So our ability to be creative is intrinsic. The life that exudes light will be a life that uses creativity to accomplish the mission. Creative power is already in us to make it happen. Our good works are accomplished when we freely operate in creative power.

Chapter 15
Shine Courageously

Most, if not all of us, at one time or another has felt courageous. Perhaps, it was that day in third grade when you had to stand up for yourself against the playground bully. Or the day the doctors returned with an unfavorable report on the condition of your health. Perhaps, your courageous moment was the day when you arrived at the office to find a pink slip on your desk. In those moments, you surely had to be courageous. You had to find strength to endure what seemed to be the hardest moment in your life.

Chances are, you can recall many of those moments when you had to be courageous. Then again, there are some moments that you can recall when you were not as courageous as you would have liked to be. Living a light-exuding life is a life of courage. It's a life of boldness and it's a life of bravery. This is no time for being scared or afraid. To become the bright shining light you were created to be, you have to be courageous. Needless to say, in order to remain vibrant and continue to shine the divine hues in the world, we have to remain courageous. To be courageous is to punch fear in the face. Light-shining lives are those who act against fear—they act courageously.

I once met a woman who stated, "I've spent my entire life in church and have never stood to testify of the Lord's goodness." I wonder how many of us have the same, if not similar, testimony. We spent years hearing of God's goodness and experiencing it, yet we never stand to tell anyone about it. Amidst the darkness of a room, it would seem hopeless that one little light could make such a difference. But it can. It takes courage to live a 100-watt life.

Living the 100-watt life requires that we act *against* fear and not *out* of fear. We shine our lights regardless of the consequences we may face in the world. Those who desire and seek to live a light-exuding life are committed to living on purpose. It takes courage to do this. Amidst the darkness of this world, it would seem easier to go with the flow and to settle in to the status quo. However, courageous lights are those that will shine even in the darkest of places.

Only those who are afraid or driven by fear will try to hide or conceal the light. The aforementioned lady was afraid to testify because she had was discouraged by those around her. She suffered with what so many suffer at the hands of oftentimes other light bearers—discouragement. No one may have ever said one word of discouragement directly to her. But perhaps their less than genuine acts or snide looks made her afraid.

Living a light-exuding life requires that we be as courageous soldiers summoned for battle. Those soldiers are confident and courageous at their call. They are excited to have been called and they are ready to do battle for their cause. They exhibit a high degree of courage and this courage keeps them moving forward. You and I too have to be courageous, shining our lights wherever we go. We cannot become fearful of man's retribution or his rebuke. Whatever we do, we cannot let the light go out. We must be courageous lights.

Chapter 16
Focused Light

As a child, I lived in a home that was poorly wired. There were some days when the slightest blow of the wind would send the house into complete darkness. Yet, there were other days when the inconsistency of energy would have portions of the house in dimly lit conditions. Have you ever seen a structure that had lighting issues? It wasn't that the lights were out; they were just inconsistent. The inconsistent flow of energy was causing brown outs.

It is often the inconsistent flows of energy that will cause us to have brown outs, surges and possibly lead to blackouts. Living a life that exudes light means that you are committed to remain focused. One of the most debilitating issues facing many of us is that of "broken focus." For reasons unbeknownst to us, we cannot remain singularly focused on any particular task. This is true especially for tasks that require extended amounts of time and energy. There is seemingly an unseen adversary that works against us in the area of remaining focused.

There are demonic, negative forces that use schemes and vices to tempt us into sin. While there are those who contend that "the devil made me do it," that is far from the truth. The demonic and negative forces can never *make* us do anything. These forces simply present to us what we like and we choose to give in to this temptation.

The Biblical writings found in James 1:14 provide the remedy to this problem. There the writer states, *But every man is tempted, when he is drawn away of his own lust, and enticed.*

Don't be drawn away or distracted! Seems simple enough, right? The dark, negative, demonic forces come into our lives with distractions that, if we allow, can draw our eyes, mind and heart away from our task of shining. Once the forces have succeeded at this, we are then enticed with worldly pleasures that lead us away from our assignment and purpose.

Let's look at the story of the Biblical figure Peter. Here is a guy destined for greatness. He preached the initial sermon after Christ's ascension into Heaven and the promise had come. He was positioned to shine. Yet, this same guy earlier on had issues with focus. He was permitted by Jesus to get out of his boat and to walk on the water. Yet, after walking on the water for a short time, he began to sink. After he walked just a few steps on the water, he lost it. But, why?

Perhaps his feet began to feel the temperature of the water. Maybe the excitement of the moment seemed to be too much. Yet biblical writings tell us that, *when he saw the wind boisterous, he was afraid.* Peter lost focus. Peter took his eyes off what mattered most and the result was a near-death experience; he began to sink. Leading a light-exuding life requires that we remain focused on what and who matters most. In case you haven't discovered it by now, our source for the light that we exude is God. Therefore, our focus must remain on the source. Our task as light bearers is to remain focused and refuse to submit to the distractions that will come in our lives. We have been permitted and commissioned to shine. Now that we have been unconstrained to shine, we must remain focused.

As a young Christian, I wanted to be able to pray and fast for hours as the older, seasoned saints did. It was the hardest thing for me to do. Every time I sat down to read and pray, something or someone would come and distract me. I remember the first time I attempted fasting; it was a sad situation. That day seemed to be filled with the aromas and smells of delicious foods that I enjoyed. The fast didn't even last an hour before I was face first in a plate of chili cheese fries. I got distracted.

To live a life that exudes light, we must understand that we have the right to remain focused. If we resist evil, it will flee. All the more, we understand that there is no temptation so great that we don't have a way of escape. We have a choice to remain focused or not.

I love police dramas and often get a kick out of the police officers reading a criminal their Miranda Rights. A police officer informs a United States citizen that, under the order of the United States Constitution, at time of arrest, he or she has the right to remain silent. We have the right to remain focused. Similar to the arresting of the citizen, we sometimes find our minds arrested or tempted by the schemes and vices of evil. Despite the attempt to seize our minds, we must remember that, as light bearers, we have rights and no demonic or negative forces can overtake you unless you yield to its power. So, we can conclude that we have the right to remain focused and free from any and all distractions. This will enable us to live a light-exuding life.

Light is focused and unwavering. We should be this way also. Whenever light is turned on in a room, the focus and aim of the light is to delete darkness. What one lamp cannot do, another can make up for. Light-exuding lives are lives that know, appreciate and illuminate focus. It's not that we are not tempted, but we recognize that the temptation is not worth losing our light. The light that we exude comes from a creative source that is able to make a way of escape for us out of any situation. Stay focused.

Chapter 17
Shine Forgiveness

Some time ago, I went through a situation that rocked me to my core. I found myself walking around with so much unforgiveness in my heart. The circumstances surrounding my unforgiving heart are not as important as the process that I had to go through to be freed from unforgiveness and go on to live a light-exuding life. I call the process the Pathway from my Head to my Heart.

Over the years, I believed that forgiveness was a key that, when presented to an offender, sets the giver free. I recognize that it's so hard to forgive someone who has done an injustice to you. It's a tough task to forgive someone who has wronged you. Sometimes, it seems as if it is just downright unfair to forgive someone who did so much wrong to you. It's even more challenging when the offender is someone close to us.

One writer stated, *It is not an enemy who reproaches and taunts me--then I might bear it; nor is it one who has hated me who insolently vaunts himself against me--then I might hide from him. But it was you, a man my equal, my companion and my familiar friend. We had sweet fellowship together and used to walk to the house of God in company. (Psalm 55:12 AMP)*

Forgiveness is the only way to be free to enjoy life again. It's the only way that you can exude light. You must work to change your impossible situation into an IM-POSSIBLE! In the end, forgiving others will do more for you than it could ever do for the one who wronged you.

Most, if not all, have experienced hurt, pain or offence. Many have been called names by people who dislike them for whatever reason. You have been unjustly labeled by those who barely knew you. Perhaps, you have been overlooked for a promotion on the job because the boss doesn't care for your personality. Maybe your husband became addicted to pornography and now prefers the visual stimulation over you. Your spouse had an affair and now you feel as though you cannot let go of the hurt and the pain that you feel. Aside from the aforementioned hurts, there are the deeply rooted areas of hurt. Your father was absent for the majority of your childhood. Your mother was a woman who used harsh words when she chastised you. Or maybe, the minister of the church molested, fondled or took advantage of you. That relationship you thought would never come to an end did, and now you are left to pick up the pieces and begin again. Wounds can leave you fuming, bitter, discouraged and even vengeful. If you are to lead a light-exuding life, you must begin the journey of the Pathway from the Head to the Heart.

INSIDE MY HEAD

Forgiveness is not a feeling or simple words you recite. It is, however, a decision. Most people have a hard time with forgiveness because it requires a change of the mind. As you journey down the pathway from your head to your heart, consider the implications and actions of your mind.

It's easy to hold on to unforgiveness. The hurt can linger for hours, days and even years. Although the initial incident is over, the thought of what happened remains persistent in your mind. The hurt and pain of the experience remains trapped in the file cabinets of your mind.

Our minds were given to us by God at the time of creation. They serve a distinct purpose in our lives and oftentimes, the mind is the starting point for everything we do in life. The mind is the starting point of all action and communication, and can therefore impact the quality of our lives. Our minds analyze information, often trying to determine how we get into the situations we find ourselves in. *How did I get hurt?*

Why was I hurt?

Who caused the hurt?

When did the hurt occur?

What was happening when I got hurt?

Once the information has been taken in, the mind converts it into familiarity. Our minds process those unanswered questions for the purpose of creating familiarity. Because it is our mind, the answers to these questions will more than likely bring added continuity to what we already feel. The answers are influenced by our emotions, reasoning and intellect. Finally, these familiarities lead and guide our actions.

We continue to struggle and cannot break free from the hurt because the actions of our minds lead us back to the place where we were hurt. Recollecting about when I endured hurt in my life, I remember being years away from the incident, yet still feeling like I was in that moment. My mind couldn't grasp the concept of forgiving those who hurt me. Every time I observed something similar to the hurt I had experienced, my mind was triggered and thus began the process that I have come to call the "pulling of the file."

THE PULLING OF THE FILE

I've worked in Corporate America for most of my adult life. In this environment, there are times when I have to pull a client's file for various purposes. Considering that I have worked with thousands of clients, seen hundreds of names, and even more phone numbers, sometimes I have to pull the file to recall the business relationship with the client. Pulling the file allows me to remember things about the client, consider my next steps, and it helps me formulate my communication with the client.

The same is true of the mind. Our minds can be triggered by smells, feelings, emotions, observations and touch. Think about when you come into your home and you are met with the awesome smell of fresh laundry. If you're like me, you may revert back in your mind to a childhood memory of playing in the clothes while your parent was trying to fold them. Perhaps, you are able to replay the feeling of the touch from the warm laundry. Or maybe, it's just the beautiful thought of time with your mother. What you experience in instances like this is the "pulling of the file" process.

The same is true with unforgiveness. In our minds, we replay what happened, how we felt, where the incident occurred and how we were impacted. What happens next is where this act becomes problematic. We must make a decision as to how we will use the information we have just retrieved. How will our actions and communication be impacted?

While I can't speak for you, I know that I have made poor decisions as to how I will respond to the "pulling of the file." Oftentimes, I have grabbed the file and its contents, and brought it from the past to the present. I left the proverbial file room of the past and brought it back to my workspace of the present. You may have done it, too. Just like the smell of the fresh laundry, the memory of being hurt changes my current mood, emotions, actions and communications. In this instance, I have made the decision to bring all the pain, all the hurt and all the emotion of my past to the present. The reason this was so easy to do is because my head has not forgiven.

Living a light-exuding life requires that I practice forgiveness. But before I can do that, I have to make a decision. To be free from unforgiveness, you must first make a decision in your mind that you will not be held hostage to the hurt, pain and anger of the past. It means you will make a conscience, voluntary decision not to harbor resentment and unforgiveness. But, that's only half of the battle.

INSIDE THE HEART

I used to think that forgiveness meant me coming into agreement with what happened to me or with the person who wronged me. I used to feel that if I forgave them, I was in fact condoning their behavior and inviting them to do it again. On the contrary, forgiveness is not about disregarding the hurtful actions caused by the offender. Forgiveness is about me freeing myself of the negative feelings, sensitivity, perceptions and emotions of what happened. When we forgive, we are not denying that the act, deed or offence hurt us. Nor does forgiveness free the offender of accountability of their actions. Forgiveness releases us to move on with life in peace.

In most situations, forgiveness is a decision to let go of the bitterness, bile, anger and thought of reprisal. This is a tough pill to swallow given the fact that sometimes the act that hurt you remains a permanent fixture in your daily life. Something or someone may serve as a constant reminder of what happened. Therefore, our decision to forgive is also an act of boldness to face the situation that offended you. The boldness to face the situation will decrease its clench and help move you down the pathway to encouragement.

Forgiveness is the act of releasing the past to embrace the future. When I forgive, I am relinquishing my hostility of the past for the enjoyment of my future. Furthermore, forgiveness allows you to move on with your life, placing the act, place or person who hurt or offended you further away from your present state of mind and affairs. However, when we don't forgive, we remain tied to that moment where the hurt or offence occurred. Unforgiveness keeps that experience alive within you and it causes you to miss out on the present day's joy. This becomes a weight; it stifles your growth and it cripples your emotions. It zaps your energy. These are just the natural side effects.

Spiritually, you become bitter. Bitterness is fueled by unforgiveness. A biblical writer said it like this, *Lest any root of bitterness springing up trouble you, and thereby many be defiled* (Hebrews 12:15). The root of bitterness will trouble us spiritually and cause us to fail. Unforgiveness becomes such a heavy burden to bear. It can lead you to a pathway of destruction and devastation. However, forgiveness can lead you to the path of well-being. This well-being is four-fold: body, soul, mind and spirit.

I wasn't really prepared for the forgiveness journey. I endured a hurt and offence that left me paralyzed and feeling incapable of moving on in my life. I was angry, sour, bitter, frustrated, vengeful and even self-destructing. I was prepared to harm myself and others because the hurt was so deep. The offence ruled my life for months and even years. I couldn't seem to shake the emotions, the feelings and the sensitivity. No matter what I did, the pain would not go away. Reliving that instance was only making my life worse. I thought if I talked about the situation over and over again, it would build some type of antidote that would cure me. Instead, the constant rehashing of the matter only fueled my anger, rage and unhappiness. I became a prisoner to my own thoughts and emotions, and I unknowingly was the only person holding the key to my deliverance. Soon, my emotions became terribly unstable. The sights, sounds and smells sent me into a tail spinning rage because they reminded me of the offence. The reason I couldn't get over the hurt, pain and offence was because every time I regurgitated the experience in my mind, my thoughts or writings, I was giving life to it. I was asking my pain, hurt and offence to live, while I slowly died.

While the mind is the hub for thoughts and the place where all actions start, our heart is an important part to the process. Living a light-exuding life requires you to make the decision with your mind to forgive. Confession is made with the mouth, but we believe with our hearts. Forgiveness is a two-part process that requires the mind to make a decision and the heart to believe the decision. Once this process has begun, your life will change. I'm a living witness. I feel a thousand times better since I've forgiven.

Light-exuding lives will always strive to operate in forgiveness. Light-exuding lives are quick to forgive and slow to harbor resentment. Let's focus on shining forgiveness over the world.

Chapter 18
Living with Light

Rev. Dr. Martin Luther King, Jr. said, "Darkness cannot drive out darkness; only light can do that." We have been given the power to light up the dark areas of our world. Our lives have been placed in this world as lights upon a light stand, purposed to provide light to the world around us.

Many struggle with the thought of being light in the world. One of the major reasons we struggle is the fear of being alone. Living a light-exuding life will, in most instances, lead us to a place of solitude. It's in that place that we often become familiar with our true self. This can be a frightening experience. We have become inter-reliant persons, which was placed in us at our creation. However, this sometimes becomes a problematic trait to our lives because we refuse to go at some things alone. The decision to shine is a personal decision to be made with or without the support of others. Living a light-exuding teaches you that you don't need a team for everything.

During his earthly ministry, when Jesus spoke about those who wished to follow Him, He shared with them what was required. He told them that a man must take up his cross and follow. That was the prerequisite. The cross represents the place of death, self-denial, coming together and elevation. The same is true for us who want to live a light-exuding life. We must face the reality of where we are. Then, we must realize that there is a need for light. To live a light-exuding life, we must personally make up our minds to bear our proverbial cross and shine. Although our living of the light-exuding life will attract others and we will collaborate with others, the starting point is a place of individualism.

WHY WE MUST BE LIGHT

Many of the people we see daily are in the fight of their lives. The struggles are great and varied. Some are challenged beyond what we could ever imagine and these challenges have them ready to throw in the towel and quit. You and I have to be the light that shines in their lives. They need your light!

Chapter 19
Like. Comment. Share.

The emergence of social media sites like Twitter®, Facebook®, Instagram® and Pinterest® has caused many to question whether or not we've become too social. The day of waiting to call a new contact once you've reached the office or home has longed ended. I recall many times when I have literally been in front of audiences, secular and religious, giving a speech and my electronic device notifies me of a friend request or new follower request from someone who is present in the room.

When this happens, I'm often excited and hoping that it is because my speech is so moving and intriguing that they want to connect immediately. However, sometimes I'm alarmed at how fast people want me to call them a friend via social media sites.

Occasionally, I feel the emergence of these technologies has presented an insurmountable number of challenges as well as advantages. The challenge with privacy seems to be paramount of them all. Yet, the advantages of being able to network with people that maybe you've met in person once is exciting. For the light bearers at large, the advantage is boundless.

Some of today's leading technology firms, business analysts and now a growing number of once conservative Christians agree that the growing trend in sharing your faith and light centers on the use of technology. Churches now have apps for their membership. We are seeing reports of record numbers of persons tuning into religious services via the Internet. Religious leaders from the highest of positions have turned to social media sites as an opportunity to share their messages of hope, love and salvation.

The challenge facing many light bearers is the desire to share their light. While there is no right or wrong way to share, much is to be said about what we share and how much of it we share. It is an exciting thing to share your newfound happiness in life with others. Even more, it is a requirement that you share your light. For most of us, this is an atypical response and you desire to share what new things you've experienced and learned with others. However, the challenge is often how and when to begin.

Start with the light. Our everyday life becomes the medium by which we share our faith, good works and the light. We are living letters to be read of all men. Our lives exude the light before men and they are able to see our good works. The hope is that they inquire of the source of our light and we tell them from whence it came. Our lives become the beacon of light by which others are led to the light. Our display is not merely a placeholder, but instead an indicator of the change available to others.

Living out the principles highlighted in this book will lead others to know and want to know about our faith, our beliefs and our light. The world is attracted to light and when the light is vibrant and consistent, they will desire to know more about it. The goal of the light bearer is to become a consistent, vibrant light in the world by exuding the divine hues all around.

Epilogue
God First

Some people in the world choose to praise and worship creation. They acknowledge and give reverence to the animals, trees, plants and all other pieces of the world around them. While, I recognize the beauty of creation and the awesomeness of its existence, I'm challenged with offering praise and worship to it. The creation that we see today is because God created it. So to praise the creation and not the Creator is unjust and imbalanced. You must acknowledge the Creator.

Living a light-exuding life is beyond our own personal fulfillment and happiness. This life transcends our very existence in the world. To live a 100-watt life, you must put God first in your life. No person, place or thing can come before Him. Our spouses, houses, careers, ambitions or dreams have to all take a backseat to God. My late grandmother was known for her quick responses and use of scripture in her everyday conversations. Most often, she was heard reciting Matthew 6:33: *But seek ye first the kingdom of God, and his righteousness; and all these things shall be added unto you.*

She recited this passage so often that it became etched into the memory of most, if not all of her family. My grandmother understood that no matter what we set out to accomplish, it had to begin with God. Reverend Patricia Beall Gruits, a noted preacher, lecturer and author wrote in her book *Understanding God,* " God is the only one wise enough and strong enough to create and maintain the earth and universe." The author's observation and point gives us more reason to begin with God. To ensure that the light that shall exude from our lives remains bright and exuberant, we must start with God.

All the more, considering the author's statement, we see a notable characteristic about God. That characteristic is that He does nothing temporarily. When God decides to do something, He has already made provisions for the past, present and future. Whatever he does, He plans to maintain. Therefore, we see just how essential it is to seek God first and thereby have the right foundation. As we endeavor to live light-exuding lives, we must know the foundation upon which we build. There is no building that remains in existence today if it was built from the top down. The same is true with those who reach natural or spiritual success of any magnitude. There must always be a foundation. It would befit us to have a solid foundation that we can build upon. We are told to ensure that our foundation is solid before we build, or else our structures will fall because of the elements in which we live. *(Luke 6:48-49)* Our solid foundation, upon which we build our lives, has to be God and His truths. Attempting to build upon fleshly desires, ambitions, finances or material gains will only lead to great ruins.

I once heard a quote that said that your vision or dream must be so big that it cannot exist apart from God. If the life that you're trying to live can be done without God, I must inform you that it's temporary. Much of what we call success today are really temporary accomplishments. The likelihood of that accomplishment lasting beyond our lifetime is next to nothing. God desires for us to have a light that is everlasting. If the light that we show forth is temporal, it is not the light of God. Don't live with counterfeit, temporal lighting. If you are reading this and have been attempting to live a light-exuding life without God, you can change that. As you're reading, this very moment is your opportunity to get in right connection (relationship with God) and receive His light to experience the 100-watt life. Similar to a race, we run the race of life and the objective is to reach the end. However, one of the key components that make a race a race is the starting point. While we may not all travel the same speed in the race, we all have the same starting point in it. As it is in the natural, so it is in the spirit. The starting place for all is God. The desire to lead a 100-watt life reveals to us the need for a real relationship with the Lord Jesus Christ. A bulb in an unconnected socket is useless. When we truly get connected, we can shine. We cannot afford to be frivolous with our lights. Seek divine connection.

THE PRAYER OF SALVATION

Salvation through Jesus Christ is available to whosoever will. I thank God for you taking the time to read this book. I pray that something within this work has provided you with strength, vigor and encouragement to continue on in this race to follow Christ. All the same, I understand that you may be reading this book and have not accepted the Lord Jesus Christ as your personal savior and I want to present to you the opportunity to do so right now. Pray this prayer:

Lord Jesus, come into my heart. Lord I repent and turn from all of my sins and all of my unrighteous behavior. Lord, I ask that you create in me a clean heart and renew a right spirit within me. Lord, I confess with my mouth the Lord Jesus Christ and I believe in my heart that you have raised Jesus from the dead. Lord, I believe that you will return to this earth to gather those who have confessed you that we may live in eternity with you in heaven. Lord, I am sorry for my actions, words, thoughts, and emotions that have been contrary to your will. Lord, save me right now, in Jesus' name! Amen!

If you prayed that prayer to God with sincerity and in faith, the bible says that you have just been saved and born again. You are set free from the bondage of sin! I encourage you to find a bible-based church and join it if you have not already done so. Even if you already know the Lord as your savior, and this prayer has served as a reminder of your commitment to God, I encourage you to remain faithful in the call that God has placed on your life.

About the Author

ANTOINE JACKSON, author of *When You've Had Enough*, is a minister, author and entrepreneur. He holds a Bachelor of Arts in Business Administration. A chosen minister of God, Antoine is a powerful messenger of the Gospel of Jesus Christ. Eight years after hearing it, he acknowledged his calling and began daily works to make full use of his anointing and appointing. He preached his first public sermon in April of 2005 at the age of twenty titled, "Get Up Quickly; Change is Happening." Now an ordained Elder in the Church of God in Christ, Inc., he has been commissioned by God to reach lost souls of this world. Jackson was reared in the things of God, attending church with his grandmother and aunt in Detroit. Through this exposure, he discovered a love relationship with the Lord Jesus Christ and works daily to maintain its harmony.

For speaking engagements or to order additional copies of this book, please visit www.AntoineJackson.org.

KEEP THE LIGHT SHINING!

BLOG
antoinejackson.blogspot.com

FACEBOOK
facebook.com/authorantoinejackson

TWITTER
@ElderADJackson

YOUTUBE
Youtube.com/ministeradjackson

#100WATTLIFE

Antoine Jackson, provided **Madonna University's Bridging Lost Gaps (BLG)** program with a vision of **what are you truly living for, and what are you willing to die for.** Our students and staff truly learned that leaving a legacy is important as African American males in the 21st century. Jackson's ambitious journey beginning from a very young age illustrated a sound commitment to our students.

Our students **are more inspired to** not only attempt university studies, but **more determined to finish** university studies. Min. Jackson truly opened the minds of our students, and into a world where they can explore even more of why obtaining a four year degree is important. His **motivation, delivery, and confidence incentivizes the community to never give up.** Madonna University is truly grateful for the presence of Antoine Jackson.

— Bryant Lamar George
Director, The Bridging Lost Gaps Program (BLG),
Office of Diversity and Multicultural Affairs
Madonna University, Livonia, MI

"Flip the switch. Change the bulb. What ever you do, make up your mind to shine." - Antoine Jackson, 100-Watt Life, 2013

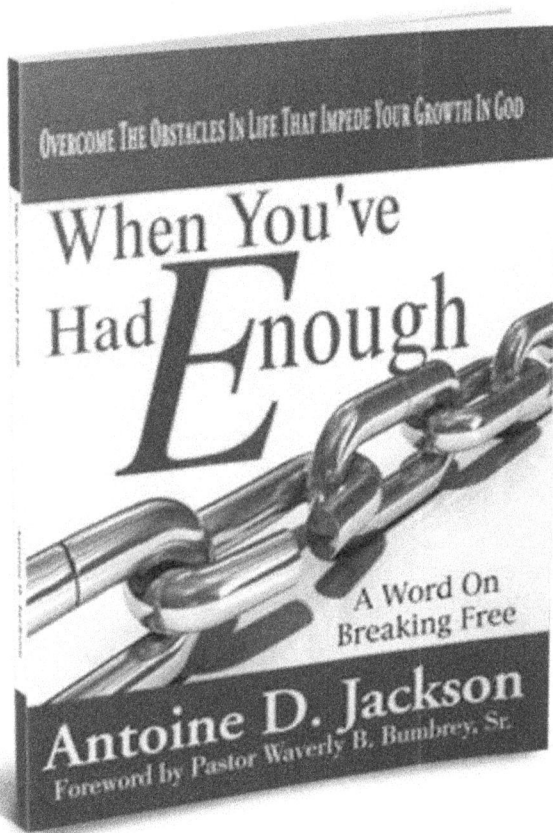

STOP LIVING BELOW THE SURFACE OF YOUR POTENTIAL. MAKE THE DECISION TO BREAK FREE.

Available at bookstores everywhere, Amazon.com® or at **AntoineJackson.org**

www.ingramcontent.com/pod-product-compliance
Lightning Source LLC
Chambersburg PA
CBHW062002040426
42447CB00010B/1870